For Yan — SG
For Joyce and Peter with love — SA

First published in Great Britain in 1999 by Macdonald Young Books,
an imprint of Wayland publishers Ltd
61 Western Road
Hove
East Sussex
BN3 1JD

Find Macdonald Young Books on the internet at
http://www.myb.co.uk

Concept and design by Liz Black
Commissioning Editor Dereen Taylor
Editor Rosie Nixon
Language Consultant Betty Root
Science Consultant Dr Carol Ballard

Text © Sam Godwin
Illustrations © Simone Abel
Book © Macdonald Young Books
M.Y.Bees artwork © Clare Mackie

A CIP catalogue record for this book
is available from the British Library

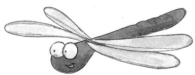

ISBN 07500 2655 3

Printed and bound in Asa, Portugal

The Trouble with Tadpoles

A first look at the life cycle of a frog

The Trouble with Tadpoles

A first look at the life cycle of a frog

Sam Godwin

MACDONALD YOUNG BOOKS

It's spring and a tiddly tadpole swims around the pond.

Where did the tadpole come from?

A tadpole starts life inside a tiny egg.

The eggs are called frog spawn. They're wrapped in a special kind of jelly.

Did someone say jelly? Yum, yum.

Lots of these eggs float together in the weeds.

The egg slowly hatches and a tiny tadpole wriggles into the water.

Fancy some tadpoles for tea?

It hides in the weeds where it feels safe.

Leave that tadpole alone, you big bully!

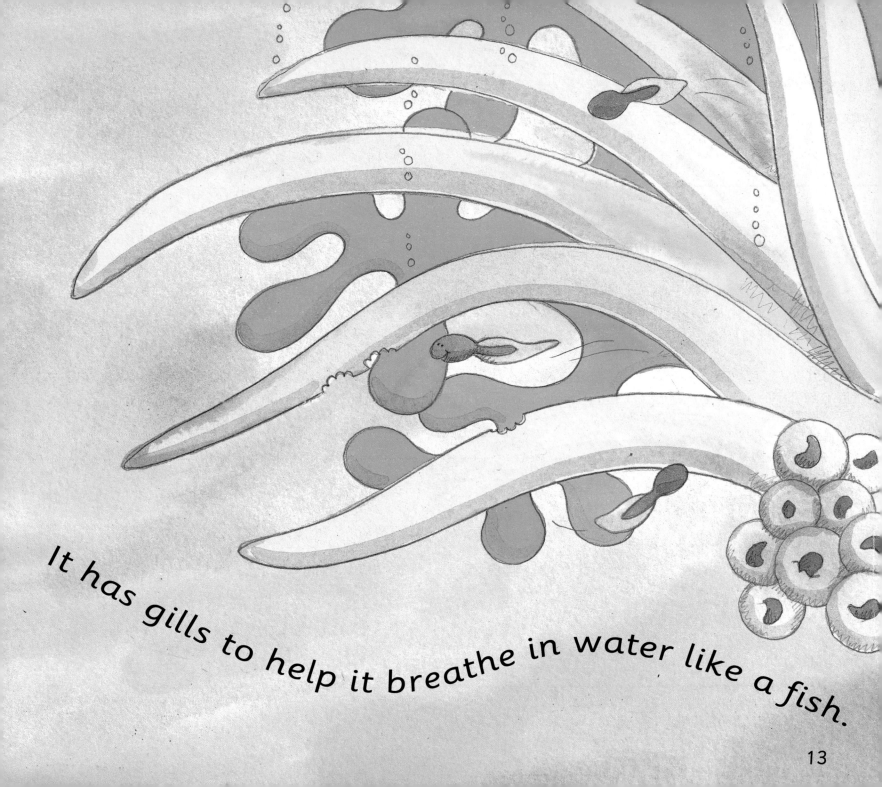

It has gills to help it breathe in water like a fish.

13

The tadpole starts to grow two legs.

Soon, the tadpole starts to grow two front legs.

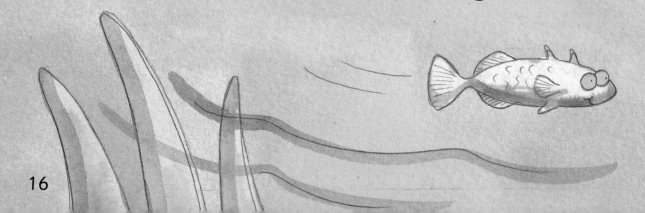

The tadpole has changed inside too – it's grown lungs and can breathe on land, just like us.

Its tail begins to get smaller and smaller.

At last the tadpole is not a tadpole anymore.

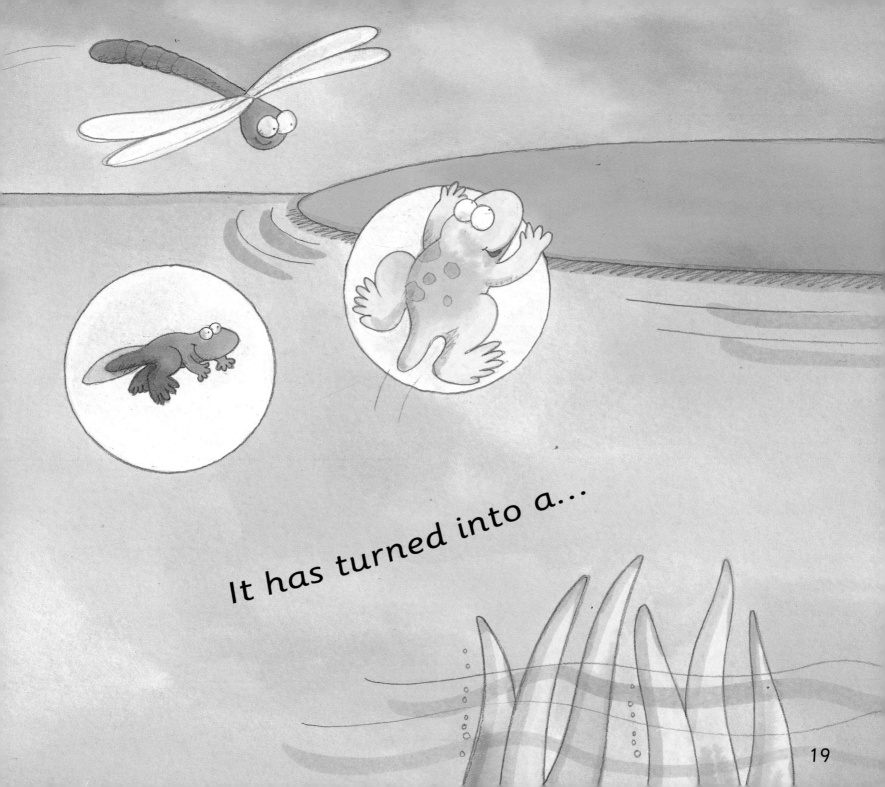

It has turned into a...

19

21

The baby frog grows fast. It learns to croak,

jump and catch flies with its long tongue.

Grown-up frogs make their home in the grass

We like to live where it's nice and damp.

but they always stay close to water.

In spring, grown-up frogs return to the pond.

The mummy frogs lay spawn in the weeds.

In no time at all, the spawn hatches and

new tadpoles are born.

Useful words

Frog spawn
A mass of frog's eggs or tiny baby tadpoles wrapped in a layer of jelly. This jelly protects and provides food for them.

Gills
The part of a fish or tadpole that helps it to breathe under water. They look like small wings and can be seen on either side of a tadpole's head.

Lungs
The part of animals and humans that helps them to breathe out of water. They cannot be seen as they are inside the body, usually in the chest.

Croak
The low, echoey sound that some frogs make.

Hatch
When a baby bird or fish wriggles out of the egg in which it started life.

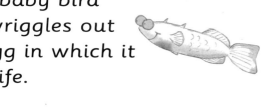

The Frog Life Cycle

⑨ Adult frogs are ready to lay more spawn.

⑧ The frog's tail disappears completely.

① Frogs lay spawn in the weeds.

⑦ The tadpole's lungs are fully grown, so it can breathe on land.

② A baby tadpole hatches out of each egg and clings to the weeds.

⑥ The tadpole grows front legs. Its mouth is quite wide. Its tail shrinks.

③ The tadpole has outside gills like a fish. After a few days it starts to feed on weeds.

⑤ The tadpole starts to grow back legs. It also starts to develop lungs.

④ The tadpole loses its outside gills. It now has gills inside its head.